SHORT BLACKS are gems of recent
Australian writing – brisk reads that quicken
the pulse and stimulate the mind.

SHORT BLACKS

REGIONS OF THICK-RIBBED ICE

HELEN GARNER

SHORT BLACKS

Published by Black Inc.,
an imprint of Schwartz Publishing Pty Ltd
37–39 Langridge Street
Collingwood VIC 3066 Australia
enquiries@blackincbooks.com
www.blackincbooks.com

First published in *The Feel of Steel*, Picador, 2001.
This edition published 2015.

National Library of Australia Cataloguing-in-Publication entry :
Garner, Helen, 1942– author. Regions of thick-ribbed ice / Helen
Garner. 9781863957663 (paperback) 9781925203509 (ebook)
Short blacks ; no.4. Professor Molchanov (ship) Voyages and travels.
Antarctica–Anecdotes.
919.8904

Cover and text design by Peter Long.

HELEN GARNER has written novels,
short stories, screenplays and many
acclaimed works of journalism. She was
the recipient of the 2006 Melbourne
Prize for Literature. Her books include
Monkey Grip, *The Children's Bach*,
Joe Cinque's Consolation, *The Spare Room*
and *This House of Grief*.

They say that tourist ships to Antarctica, even more than ordinary human conveyances, are loaded down with aching hearts. Deceived wives and widowers, men who've never been loved and don't know why, Russian crew forced to leave their children behind for years at a time, grown women who've just buried a beloved parent, people with cancer travelling to the cold before they die. They say people come here looking for 'solace'. And then there are the married couples: how calm the old ones, how eager the new! – but isn't a couple the greatest mystery of all?

*

The hats. Oh, they're terrible. One woman broaches the deck pulling on a thing like a sponge-bag, made of purple polypropylene. A little old lady is wearing a grey wool bonnet straight out of a Brueghel painting. A young bloke in spectacles sports a cap of multi-coloured segments, topped with a twirl and several small silver bells.

My own headgear, a hideous borrowed job featuring red earmuffs and a peak, is still stuffed into a corner of my suitcase, down in cabin no. 521 which I'm there to share with a perfect stranger called Robyn (and I've forgotten my earplugs).

So far, an hour after we've disembarked from Ushuaia, an Argentine port in Tierra del Fuego, I am still stubbornly refusing to believe in the cold, though my fingers have shrunk so thin that my wedding ring keeps sliding off, and my eyes and nose are streaming. *If you fall overboard*, states the Lonely Planet Guide grimly, *you will die*. I'm not the Antarctic type. I'm hanging out for a short black. I'm not adventurous, and I'm too sad to be sociable with strangers.

Stop whingeing. As the late summer Saturday afternoon draws on, we chug down the Beagle Channel, a body of calm water that splits the bent nib of South America into Chile and Argentina. The channel lies along a row of harsh, impossibly sparkling-topped mountains, each with its diaphanous scarf of cloud. Our ship is the *Professor Molchanov* out of Murmansk in the former Soviet Union, where, they say, scores of ships lie at anchor, unused, unwanted, rusting – the detritus of empire. Our crew is Russian; our captain, though only thirty-eight, is an ice-master.

'I look young,' he says, 'but I am old inside.'

He is also, various women agree later in the bar, 'a dish'.

'Haven't you taken a seasick pill yet, Helen?' asks Terry, a vet from Brisbane. 'Take one. Take it *now*.'

I obey. By 8 p.m. I am nodding off at the dinner table among my fellow adventurers, most of them shy, many of them older than

I am. In the early hours of Sunday morning we turn out of the Channel and into the Drake Passage – where, while everyone but the crew is sound asleep, we hit a force-seven gale which will rage unabated for two days and nights.

The pills knock out nausea, but the simplest tasks – going to the lavatory, getting dressed – become Herculean. Robyn and I lurch past each other in the cramped space of our cabin, flung against walls and cannoning off cupboard fronts. Somehow a lifeboat drill is achieved, after which we hibernate. Our porthole is bisected by a madly tilting grey line. I am in love with my bunk, so narrow and perfect, like the single bed of childhood.

Sometimes Ann, the *Molchanov* doctor,

materialises next to my drugged head, holding out a bottle of lemon-flavoured water, a handful of dry biscuits. Morning and evening a quiet voice comes over the tannoy into the cabin: this is Greg Mortimer, eminent mountaineer – Everest, K2 – and leader of our 'voyage'. (No one calls it a 'tour' or a 'trip', and since the storm began I have stopped seeing this as pretentious.) He has a knack of saying only what's required, without embellishment. To city people disturbed by the screaming wind, his voice is comforting. 'Sleep well,' he says at night, like a comforting, benevolent father.

By Monday evening the huge waves smooth out. People creep from their burrows. Some have, incredibly, been unperturbed, attending learned disquisitions in the bar on the habits of penguins. Other voyagers confess to having spewed in public – a great leveller. Thea, the woman in the Brueghel bonnet, shows off a carpet-burn the size of a dollar coin on her forehead. Everyone is friendlier since the storm: now we are shipmates.

Around 9 p.m. we gather on the bridge to keep vigil for our first iceberg. This far south, in February, it doesn't get dark til after eleven. The bridge is a serious place, of work and watching. The Russian officers are big blokes smelling of cigarettes, with moustaches and silver teeth, and voices that rumble from deep in their torsos. They murmur to each other, slip out on to the deck for a smoke, stand at the wheel or bend over charts spread on drawing boards. We are shy of them and keep stepping out of their way.

Out on deck the air is gaspingly cold but the evening sky is pretty, the water a steely, inky grey-blue. Suddenly there's a moon, riding tranquil between layers of bright cloud. Leaning over the rail I see my first tiny chunk of ice go bobbing past, very close to the ship's side. At once I'm seized by an urge to compare it with something – with anything: it's the size of a loosely flexed hand, palm up; like a Disney coronet with knobbed points; as hollow as a rotten tooth. For some reason I am irritated by this urge, and make an effort to control it.

Inside, the bridge is warm and dim. Thirty people stand about talking, but intent on the greying line that divides sea from sky. There it is – there's one. And another. The first iceberg is only a pale blip on the horizon. The second is greyer, straighter-sided, more 'like a building'. Night thickens as we approach them. Iceberg no.1 is unearthly, mother-of-pearl, glowing as if with its own inner light source. People grow quiet, their social chatter stills. The only sounds are the buzz and hum of the radar, the dull rumble of the engine, and out on deck the rushing of the wake.

Then somebody begins to liken the iceberg to a face. 'It's got a sad eye. See its nose?' On and on people go: it's like a sphinx, a Peke's face, an Indian head with its mouth open. Again I am secretly enraged by this, and by my own urgent desire to do the same. I stare at the iceberg as it looms two hundred metres away on our port side. It gleams with a pearly purity. It's faceted: creamy on the left, whiter on the right. It looks stable, like an island rather than something floating. Water riffles around its foot. I strain and fail to see it only in abstract terms. I don't want to keep going 'like, like, like'. But I can't stop myself.

*

On Tuesday morning we slip out of the Bransfield Strait into the misty mouth of the Antarctic Sound. While dressing I glance out the porthole and see a tremendous iceberg – big as two houses – shaped like a chunk of frozen cloud sliced off by a downward stroke of a spatula. The tilt of its top is the cleanest, most perfect line I've ever seen. Rush up on deck, rugging up as I run. The water is as flat and lumpy with ice scraps as the surface of a gin and tonic.

In the fog the monster bergs are everywhere. *Molchanov* cruises among them, gently. Each one is fissured, flawed with a wandering seam of unnatural cellophane blue-green, almost dayglo: older ice, someone explains, more densely compressed. A lump of ice needs to be only the size of, say, a small washing machine for this faery green to be present in it, like a flaw in an opal.

'Unrool, idn't it,' murmurs big Dave the diver, a Queenslander with huge square teeth.

It's hopeless, trying to control the flood

of metaphor. People cry out in wonder. Look – a temple, with pillars. The white ridged sole of a Reebok. There's one with a curved spine. Hey – an aircraft carrier! A flooded cathedral. Somebody's been at that one with a melon-baller. Suddenly, we glide into an area of small ice chunks, like the aftermath of an explosion – pieces no bigger than a folded sheet, a dish-rack, a car engine.

Exhausted with the ecstasy of it, you turn your eyes away for a moment, to rest – and the sun breaks through the cloud cover to reveal a whole further field of icebergs – great flaring blocks of perfect, piercing silver.

The fog lifts further. There it is – the Antarctic Peninsula, a continent of dark rocks, of ridged and bony snow. They want us to climb into an inflatable, flat-bottomed zodiac and *set foot* on it? My stomach rolls with excitement and fear.

I wish I didn't have to write about this. I wish I could find a silent spot and hide in it to gaze and gaze; or crawl back into my bunk and sleep off the wonder.

Instead I go to breakfast. There's bacon. You can smell it all over the ship.

*

Our first trip ashore, to Brown Bluff, is apparently to be about penguins. Urk. I've got a feather-phobia: birds revolt me. We are told that our behaviour on land must leave no trace: no 'toileting'; no food or drink; and we are strictly forbidden to take anything away, not even a shell, a stone, a tiny bone. Tubs of water will be provided on *Molchanov*'s deck for our return; we must scrub every scrap of penguin shit off our boots, or else the air inside the ship will become unbearable.

The zodiacs rise and fall at the bottom of the gangway, down which we blunder in single file, puffy in our grotesque wet-weather gear of Goretex, rubber, velcro and large coarse zips.

As we bounce across a kilometre of water towards a line of brown and white cliffs, the penguin stench hits us: shit and feathers, with an overlay of fish.

On the stony beach, people fan out with their camera equipment and become solitary. Each photographer attempts to establish an intense relationship with an individual penguin. I tiptoe past these strivings, feeling like an intruder.

I note with relief that some penguins are not waddling about on their flabby feet, or standing in forward-slanted throngs on points of land, but are lying, singly or in twos and threes, flat on their bellies on the grey rocks, their eyes closed to slits, doing nothing at all. Just loafing about. I long to emulate them. But I'm afraid even to seat myself on a rock. What if I fall asleep, or slip into an ice trance, and the zodiacs forget me and I get *left behind*?

This is of course impossible, due to a rigorously enforced system of tags, labels, life-belt counting and so on – but it's my first twinge of primal dread, mixed with a swooning sensation. I'm tired. I'm guilty about not liking penguins. I'm cold. I have to keep wiping my nose. I'm incapacitated by all these bulky clothes. I'm lonely because everyone else is hiding behind a camera. Everywhere I turn, my view is blocked by some keen bean with a tripod. I fight the sense that a person with a camera has a prior right to any view we both happen to be looking at. I am being driven insane by photography.

OK, one sub-group of the voyage is actually here to be coached by Darren, a tall quiet young professional photographer; but your average punter on board has brought at least one camera and several kilometres of film. I have left my Pentax at home. I tell incredulous shipmates that it's too old and heavy to carry, but the real reason is that at the pre-trip briefing a couple of months ago, people spoke so fanatically of bringing a back-up camera in case their main one fell overboard or got splashed in the zodiac that it brought out the party-pooper in me. I determined on the spot that I would go to the icy continent in a state of heroic lens-lessness; that I would equip myself with only a notebook and a pen.

But I forgot something. The cold.

Two degrees Celsius doesn't sound that scary, specially if you've been reading about Shackleton's journey in the open boat, or Apsley Cherry-Garrard's *Worst Journey in the World* – tales in which temperatures of seventy below scarcely raise an eyebrow. Still, the expedition guides urge us over and over again to take the cold seriously, to dress in layers against it, to keep dry, to wear several pairs of gloves. I have brought cotton ones, wool ones, and a pair of mittens made of stiff stuff like leather. Have you ever tried to take notes wearing boxing gloves?

With my huge bulging paws I wrestle the notebook and pen out of my pocket and start describing things, partly to justify my presence, partly to keep from falling asleep: 'Penguins: ridiculous, helpless-looking creatures, always in a flap. A penguin looks like a person trying to walk in an inverted sack; it has to strain its feet apart to keep the neck of the bag open round its ankles. The clifftops are crenellated: you expect to see the feathered heads of Indian warriors peep over them, it's like Arizona.'

Oh, shut up, smart-arse.

I stow the book and sit down gingerly on a little point of rock, out of the wind. In this bay the sound of the ocean is hushed. Further around the rocky beach stands a wall of ice. Its vertical face is snicked with tiny hollows, in each of which there lurks a droplet of the same secret, tawdry green that seamed this morning's icebergs.

A chunk of ice the size and shape of a double bed (with base) detaches itself from near the top of the wall, and floats gracefully down and out of my line of sight – slow, ethereal. But it lands with a shocking roar and a smash, and there's a fluster in the water, which dies away. Back inside the ice river there's a constant groaning and creaking, an occasional crack like a pistol shot.

Mild sun shines on my up-turned face.

None of these gargantuan cataclysms has anything to do with me. Nothing is my fault. While the ice behaves as it must, I am permitted to sit here on a rock, strangely at peace.

*

Something funny happens to time, down here. The nights are so short and the light so foreign, we're so buffeted by weather, bombarded by new sights, wrung out with wonder, that the memory starts to pack up. We lose our grip on the sequence of events. Cameras are impotent against the slippage. Our guides work late into the night to counteract it: each morning we wake to find, wedged under our cabin door-handle, a two-page account of the activities of the previous day, complete with map, and plan for the day ahead. This is not just their usual efficiency: it's protection against an attack of severe existential anxiety.

*

At the lunch table Nicola and Sue, *Molchanov* workers, relate how they lassoed a small iceberg and brought it back for cubes at the bar.

'We were hauling and hauling! It was like a birth! And suddenly there was this great big THING in the zodiac! Just as well there were no men there! If there'd been men they would've gone, "Stand back, girls! Let *me* handle this!" We were determined – we were like, "This iceberg is not going to beat us!"

The sole bloke at the table, Michael, another mountaineer, quiet, with a modest, introverted demeanour, who has lost his toes and parts of his feet to frostbite on Everest, sits looking on, half smiling.

'The food on this ship is great,' says another woman at the table, lifting her forearms off the cloth which is dampened to prevent the plates from sliding about. 'It must be the cold. – I've been eating four times my usual rations and I'm not even putting on weight!'

*

That night we sail into our second storm, force ten on the Beaufort scale. It is colossal. I hardly sleep. Never before has it been strenuous just to lie down. I'm stiff from neck to feet all night long. In daylight, speechless people stagger hand over hand along the corridors and up to the bridge, where there are rails to grip, and one grips them hard, gulping and shaking, exhilarated, scared.

The sea is a heaving grey field of waves as big as apartment blocks, which rise with majestic deliberation and smash themselves over the bridge. For a few seconds after each impact, the ice fragments cascading down the glass blot out the world, then camouflage it, abstracting it into wild patterns of white, grey and streaming loden green.

Hanging on with aching arms, flexing my knees and swaying with the madness, I begin to understand that the *Professor Molchanov* is not just a dead contraption of rivets and chunks of metal, but an entity, a living being.

It transforms into *she*. She bounds, throbs, moans. She has a sense of her own springy wholeness, as she quivers on the lip of a wave, gathering herself for the next plunge. The aliveness, the working beingness of her goes straight to the heart: I admire her, she moves me. For the first time in my life I understand how one can love a ship.

*

'My feeling of this part of Antarctica,' says Greg, 'is usually much more gentle. But this time it showed itself in a really raw way. We got a faceful.'

*

The next evening we go ashore at Half Moon Island, to inspect a penguin rookery.

While we're beaching the first zodiac, a sudden wind springs up and slashes across the bay, making the water bristle. The stones underfoot, as we scramble out of the boats and up the steep beach, are grey and clanking, big as bread-and-butter plates. Camera mania flourishes at once, obliterating all social contact: I mooch about on my own, crabby and left out.

A lone penguin, separated from its fellows, stumps along beside me on its damp pink feet. We cast an ill-tempered glance at each other. It's a companionship of sorts, I suppose. I am just starting to appreciate the pearly sheen of its dress shirt when it loses interest and staggers away behind a beautiful old clinker-built rowboat which has sagged and half collapsed on the stones.

I slog on by myself up to the saddle, where I am rewarded by a splendid vista: white peaks all crumbling down on the other side of a narrow channel, in which mad dark water is bumping with frozen lumps. The wind up here ('the cleanest air in the world') nearly bowls me over. Breathe it, Misery Guts, and let that be enough.

Way down behind me, there's a commotion at the water's edge. A bunch of tiny people is struggling to drag the second zodiac, then the third, up on to the beach. The light is weakening and the wind is growing stronger by the minute. On the crest I'm having to crouch and claw at the ground so as not to be blown off my feet. *Professor Molchanov* looks very small, out there in the bay, and awfully far away.

I scramble crab-wise down to the shore. Seven people are battling to hold the third zodiac steady. Waves are slopping over its stern, crashing and dragging at it; it's filling with water, we can't pull it up. Night's coming, there's a harsh side-on swell, and why should the wind drop?

It doesn't help that only a metre away from our struggles a single penguin is frolicking in the dark water, as carefree as if the sun were beaming down at noon. While the humans shout and haul and groan, it loops and dives and twirls, merry as an otter.

The sky is so pure it hurts to look at it. The wind whips fine grit off the stones and slashes it into our streaming eyes. My stomach knots in animal dread, a horror of cold. What if we can't launch our zodiacs?

How will we get through this night? Has *Molchanov* got another boat to save us?

At the far end of the beach we can see a clump of small huts on bare, dark scree. No lights, no sign of life – only the blue and white Argentine flag painted on the roof: Camara base. Oh God. I picture the whole gang of us having to break in, and shuddering all night in a pile on the floor of the biggest hut.

Over the wind Greg shouts at us: 'Walk around the shore to the base! We'll bring the boats across! It's calmer there!'

I set out to trudge a kilometre on the big shifting stones, my head seething with thoughts of the pathetic will I hastily scrawled the night before I left home, of bequests I made to certain people which

I now suddenly and savagely regret.

Someone shouts to me and points to a dark thing squirming among the rocks two metres away – a seal, the size of a terrier. I give it one look before the photographers descend on it with their ravening lenses. I keep stumping along in my brand-new gumboots, leaning forward and stabbing my toes among the stones, the only way to make progress against the cold wall of wind. My eyes pour liquid. I keep overtaking older couples struggling along in the same bent posture. They look up as I steam past, but in our scarves and sunglasses and headgear we don't recognise each other. We drive onwards, toes first, leaning into the wind.

Molchanov Sue has somehow got to Camara beach before us, and is talking with a big, moustachio'd Argentinian scientist in polar gear. She shouts, 'There's room for all of us to sleep here if we have to!' Straggling in, people jockey for position out of the wind behind a tiny orange hut right near the water's edge. We huddle there in a clump, giggling feebly. Here come our zodiacs, bounding across the fierce, darkening bay.

Greg has got soaked to the groin. His gumboots are full of water. He upends them, wrings out his sopping socks and stoically puts them back on to his blue feet.

A woman says to him, 'You must be freezing.'

He shrugs manfully: 'Oh – not specially ...'

'I mean your *feet* must be freezing,' she insists.

'Well . . .' he says, looking away as if embarrassed; then, in a rush: 'Oh, none of that stuff – yes! They are!'

He gives a sudden laugh and throws both arms round her in a quick hug. This guy has climbed to the roof of the world? and he mocks his own tendency to macho posturing? No wonder we all – women and men – adore him.

On the strength of his self-awareness I fight a powerful temptation to break the rules and pocket an orange pebble. I win; but my righteousness will never quite comfort me for the fact that I have not got that small bright stone, which signalled to me from among the big grey ones, and which that night I so badly wanted, and still do.

The captain has brought the ship closer in, to give us a lee. We zip splashily home. On deck, scrubbing off the penguin shit, we are already heroes to ourselves, staring-eyed, laughing a bit too wildly, half hysterical with relief and foolishness.

*

A woman asks Greg, 'Tell me the truth – were you scared?'

He shakes his head. 'No. I knew the worst that could happen was we'd get a bit wet. It's the wind that makes people panic. It's like standing under a helicopter, when everybody's shouting.'

*

'Of course we're exploiting the penguins,'

says an earnest woman from Canberra. 'A bunch of ignorant tourists staring at them as they go about their business.'

'I don't think they *feel* exploited, though,' says Greg with a straight face. 'Beautiful as they are, it's a pretty small brain.'

*

Forgive me, but I'm not here for the wild life. Of course I crane to see the seals, dumb and smooth as slugs, trailing blood-coloured shit as they slither off floes at our approach. Of course I gasp at the soaring of the giant petrels. Of course I race up on deck at the shout, 'Sperm whale! Port side!' and hang over the rail, excited by the grand dark thing heaving just below the surface and blowing with a hollow rush. And when only the rind of a whale can be seen from a following zodiac, when with a casual flip of the tail it's gone – of course with the others I groan in disappointment, and sit gripping the zodiac side in the keen wind, shrunken and shuddering with cold, heart in mouth, nose running, eyes watering, scanning scanning scanning . . .

But in my heart all I want to do is go out in the boats and look at ice. Seals, penguins and whales, to me, are only distractions from the bliss of this.

Where to find a language for these miraculous frozen forms? Couldn't there be poetry in the ship's library alongside the glossy photo books? Doesn't someone in Shakespeare wake from a dream about *regions of thick-ribbed ice*? Would Gerard

Manley Hopkins have found words for these teeming variations on surface?

On outings to Paradise Bay and to the 'city of bergs' off Pleneau Island, we learn calm from Greg, who never calls for silence but simply manifests it, sitting beside the outboard with his handbacks resting on his thighs, his eyes squinting. The minute people stop ripping and adjusting velcro, or tearing open film packets, we start to hear the sound the brash ice is making. It's whispering all around us, chinking, rustling on the gentle swell. We sit. We stare.

The colour of an iceberg, or of a glacier wall, is impossible to name. You call it white, but when you swing your eyes away and back, you see it's the most delicate, the palest and yet the greyest green. Mint? The

Nile? A no-colour. Water colour. Cloud colour. Again and again the eye returns to feast on the crumpled mystery of ice. One plumbs the word-well. The bucket comes up empty.

People whisper helpless clichés: 'magic', 'wonderland'. Not good enough. The forms are inhuman, but to name them we need the vocabulary of the body, of carpentry, dressmaking, masonry – all the beautiful crafts of people's hands. Pocked. Dimpled. Chiselled. Chamfered. Bevelled. Ruched. Frilled. Saw-toothed. Cloven. Striated, stippled, puckered, fringed, trimmed, carved, scrolled – or simply folded and scratched.

Always this urge to anthropomorphise grips us, as if the awe – or panic, or even, deep down, rage – provoked in us by a landscape without human meaning were too great to bear.

On the way back from Paradise Bay, at nightfall, sitting in a silent row along the rim of the zodiac, we pass a toppled, majestic thing – an iceberg like an immense coroneted head. Wagnerian? Arthurian? *Look on my works, ye mighty, and despair.* A monarch brought low, shamed, blinded, submerged to the temples. Resting his cold cheek among the ripples.

*

Fiercely I wish I had no prior inkling of this place, that everything I'm looking at were completely new to me. I hate movies and TV and videos. People with cameras are busybodies, writers are control freaks, spoiling things for everyone else, colonising, taming, matching their egos against the unshowable, the unsayable. I long to have come down here in a state of infantile ignorance. Is this a rebirth fantasy? Or perhaps it's what Greg means when he says, 'The power of this place quietens and humbles even the dickheads.'

*

The morning we go in the boats to Hydrurga Rocks (penguins, seals, and a particular bird which hovers, head into the ferocious wind, right next to my shoulder as I stand wobbling on the ridge, crazy with the brightness of the world and the faraway satin peaks, wanting to yell with joy), a photographer loses his grip on a white plastic bag. The wind whisks it out of his hand and away it soars, inflated, skimming the surface of the water like a big white bubble of poison. We all stand transfixed, mouths gaping with horror. Later I hear that one of the blokes has chased it in a zodiac and managed to pick it up; but the distress I felt at the sight of its escape still astonishes me.

*

On *Molchanov*'s deck after an outing, I see two men, half in jest, point their cameras at each other. Like two tired cowboys in their penguin-shit-stained wet-weather gear and boots, they thrust their lenses right into each other's faces. Stand-off.

'Go on – take it!' says one.

'I'm not taking a shot!' cries the other. 'I only want to stop *you* from taking one!'

What *is* this thing about cameras? Around them seem to constellate such deep anxieties. In spite of my bravado about going lensless, I've actually got a secret throw-away camera in my cabin, having cracked in Ushuaia ten minutes before we boarded the ship. I want to leave it hidden in a drawer because I am engaged in a battle with the terror of forgetting, which drives people to raise a camera between themselves and everything they encounter – as if direct experience were unbearable and they had to shield themselves from it, filter it through a machine, store up a silent, odourless version of it for later, rather than endure it now.

But doesn't my wretched notebook (which the wind tore out of my pocket on Hydrurga Rocks; which would have followed the airborne plastic bag if I hadn't stamped on it with my heavy boot in the nick of time) – doesn't a notebook perform the same function? Why can't we let experiences lay themselves down in us like compost, or fall into us like seeds which may put forth a shoot one day, spontaneously, as childhood memories do, in answer to the stimulus of ordinary life?

'Take it home,' says Greg, 'and plant it somewhere.'

'The morning star was over the mountain,' says a man to his wife at dawn on our last day, as *Molchanov* slides back up the flushed glass floor of the Beagle Channel, 'but I didn't photograph it.'

He is apologising to her for having missed something – but I want to kiss him, I want to shake his hand!

*

We disembark at Ushuaia in bright morning sun. There's a beech forest high up there behind the town: Greg and another mountaineer jump into a ratty old taxi and make a dash for the trees, to touch and smell foliage briefly before they set out, the same afternoon, back to the Peninsula on the last voyage of the season.

So this is the end. But towards four in the afternoon I get the strangest feeling that I have to go back to the wharf. What nonsense! How sentimental! – yet I can't stay away. I drift down there, furtive in my Patagonia jacket with its penguin motif, and to my surprise I find half a dozen shipmates rambling down to the water as well – only casually strolling, mind you, to get their land legs – merely chancing to be wandering in that direction.

We stand looking up at *Molchanov*'s clean side, a bunch of sad dags clustering on the dock. We've said goodbye to everyone in sight but we need to stay right to the end. I can't believe the way my chest muscles are being squeezed by an emotion I don't have a name for. Even hulking Dave the diver owns up to it: we hardly dare look at each other. To see strangers on board our ship, leaning over the rail in a proprietary manner as she edges out and turns to face the glistening channel, is painful – enraging. She was our ship, and we've already been replaced.

THE WAR OF THE WORLDS
NOEL PEARSON

Noel Pearson considers
the most confronting issue
of Australian history:
the question of genocide,
in early Tasmania
and elsewhere.

REGIONS OF THICK-RIBBED ICE
HELEN GARNER

Helen Garner tells the tale
of a journey to Antarctica
aboard the *Professor
Molchanov*, spanning
icebergs, tourism, time,
photography and the many
forms of desolation.

SHORT ● BLACKS

THE BRAVE ONES
EAST TIMOR, 1999
JOHN BIRMINGHAM

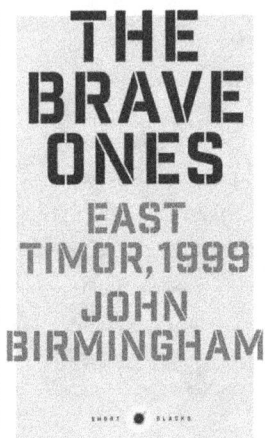

John Birmingham's unflinching account of the Indonesian Army's Battalion 745 as it withdrew from East Timor after the 1999 independence vote, leaving a trail of devastation in its wake.

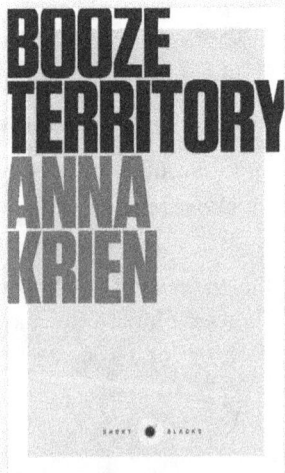

BOOZE TERRITORY
ANNA KRIEN

Anna Krien takes a clear-eyed look at Indigenous binge-drinking, and never fails to see the human dimension of an intractable problem, shining a light on its deep causes.

THE
ONE
DAY
DAVID
MALOUF

SHORT ● BLACKS

David Malouf traces the meaning of Anzac Day and shows how what was once history has now passed into legend, and how we have found in Anzac Day 'a truly national occasion.'

Prosper
A voyage at sea
Simon
Leys

SHORT ● BLACKS

Simon Leys' exceptionally beautiful and elegiac essay about a summer spent on the crew of a tuna-fishing boat in Brittany.

CYPHERPUNK REVOLUTIONARY
ON JULIAN ASSANGE
ROBERT MANNE

SHORT ● BLACKS

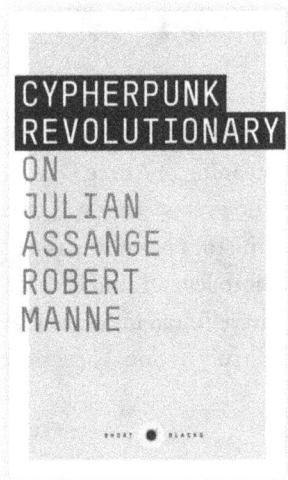

Robert Manne reveals the making of Julian Assange and shows how he became one of the most influential Australians of our time.

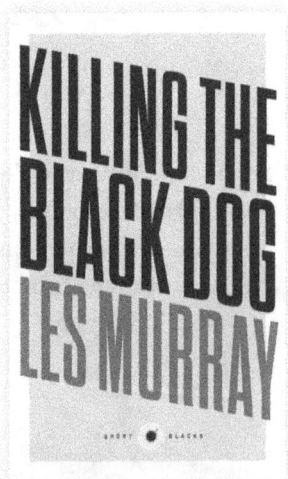

KILLING THE BLACK DOG
LES MURRAY

SHORT ● BLACKS

Les Murray's frank and courageous account of his struggle with depression.

WWW.SHORTBLACKS.COM

NO FIXED ADDRESS

ROBYN DAVIDSON

SHORT ● BLACKS

Robyn Davidson's fascinating and moving essay about nomads explores why, in times of environmental peril, the nomadic way with nature still offers valuable lessons.

TRADITION, TRUTH &

TOMORROW

GALARRWUY YUNUPINGU

SHORT ● BLACKS

Galarrwuy Yunupingu tells of his early life, his dealings with prime minsters, and how he learnt that nothing is ever what it seems.